PARIS
PAINT
BOX

NEW AND SELECTED POEMS

For Frank and Elaine,
Hoping you enjoy these poems,
With best wishes.

Helena

Helena Minton
8-30-22

HELENA MINTON

PARIS PAINT BOX

NEW AND SELECTED POEMS

Loom Press
Amesbury, Massachusetts
2022

Paris Paint Box: New and Selected Poems
Copyright © 2022 by Helena Minton

ISBN 978-0-931507-30-4
All Rights Reserved
Printed in the United States of America
First Edition

Book Design: Keith Finch
Cover painting: *The Tuileries* by Berthe Morisot (1885),
image courtesy of wikiart.org/Wikimedia Commons (public domain)
Author photograph: David DeInnocentis
Printing: Versa Press, Illinois
Typeface: Felix and Century

Loom Press
15 Atlantic View, Amesbury, Massachusetts 01913
www.loompress.com
info@loompress.com

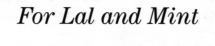

For Lal and Mint

Acknowledgments

Grateful acknowledgment is made to the editors and publishers of the original books:

Poems from *The Raincoat Colors*. Copyright 2017 by Helena Minton. Reprinted with the permission of The Permissions Company, Inc., on behalf of Finishing Line Press, www.finishinglinepress.com. All rights reserved.

The Gardener and the Bees, March Street Press, 2006.

Poems from *The Canal Bed*. Copyright 1985 by Helena Minton. Reprinted with the permission of The Permissions Company, Inc., on behalf of Alice James Books, alicejamesbooks.org. All rights reserved.

Poems from *After Curfew*, in *Personal Effects*. Copyright 1976 by Helena Minton. Reprinted with the permission of The Permissions Company, Inc., on behalf of Alice James Books, alicejamesbooks.org. All rights reserved.

Individual poems have previously appeared in the following publications, sometimes in different form.

Aspect, The Beloit Poetry Journal, The Bridge Review: Merrimack Valley Culture, The Colorado State Review, Edna, Four Corners, Green House, The Hampden-Sydney Poetry Review, The Harbor Review, Ibbetson Street Review, Karamu, The Larcom Review, The Leon Literary Review, The Listening Eye, The Lowell Review, Loom, Masspoetry.org, The Merrimack Literary Review, The Muddy River Poetry Review, The Paddock Review, Parting Gifts, Poetry, Red River Review, Renovation Journal, Route 9, Solstice Literary Magazine, Solo, Sojourner, Sou'wester, The Tower Journal, West Branch, The Wilderness House Literary Review, The Women's Review of Books, ROAR Magazine: A Journal of the Literary Arts by Women, Flowering After Frost: An Anthology of Contemporary New England. (Branden Press, 1975), Raising Lilly Ledbetter: Women Poets Occupy the Workspace (Lost Horse Press, 2015), Nasty Women Poets: An Unapologetic Anthology of Subversive Verse (Lost Horse Press, 2017), Landscapes and Legends, Selected Poems from Andover's 350th Poetry Festival, Andover, Massachusetts, 1996.

For their steadfast support and encouragement, I would like to thank my husband, David DeInnocentis; my son, Ted DeInnocentis; and my brother, Cronan Minton. For their camaraderie in poetry, and for their invaluable insights in shaping these poems, I would like to thank Kathleen Aponick; the members of the evening workshop, Kathleen Aguero, Suzanne Berger, Christopher Jane Corkery, and Erica Funkhouser; and the poets of the Skimmilk Farm workshop, Irma Haggerty, Marie Harris, Kathi Hennessey, Ellen Hersh, Karen Kilcup, Kathy Solomon, Elizabeth Knies Storm, and Cornelia Veenendaal. Thank you to Paul Marion for his attentive and thoughtful editing, and for his dedication to the advancement of literature over so many years. Thank you to Rosemary Noon for her careful reading and advice.

Contents

PART ONE
NEW POEMS

Paris Paint Box: Poems on the Life and Paintings
of Berthe Morisot

PART TWO
SELECTED POEMS

Part
ONE

NEW POEMS

PARIS PAINT BOX

Poems on the Life
and Paintings of

BERTHE MORISOT

1841–1895

Preface

Berthe Morisot was born in 1841 in Bourg, France, one of four children, in an haute bourgeoisie family. It happened to be the same year an American, John G. Rand, invented a method of preventing watercolor paint from drying out too fast and opened up the freedom for plein air painting. It has been said that she was a descendant of Fragonard. Morisot lived most of her life in Paris, with extended stays in various parts of the French countryside. She and her family endured the Siege of Paris of 1870. She studied with Camille Corot and married Eugène Manet, the brother of renowned painter Edouard. They had one child, Julie, who also became a painter. In 1874 Berthe was the only woman artist who exhibited her work at the First Impressionist Exhibition. She died in 1895. Her work sold well during her lifetime, but then faded from view. In recent years she has garnered new attention. Much of her work is in private collections. Members of the Rouart family, descendants of Julie, donated Morisot's papers and a selection of her artworks to The Musée Marmottan Monet in Paris. The art historian Jean-Dominique Rey has said, "If we had to define Berthe Morisot's originality—the quality that really distinguishes her from her contemporaries—we might describe her as a painter of the early morning light."

Note: Poem titles in italics are also the titles of paintings.

I

"... with natures like those of your daughters ... my teaching will not confer the meager talents of genteel accomplishments. They will become painters. Do you have any idea what this means?"

— Joseph Guichard to Marie Cornélie,
Berthe Morisot's mother, 1860

An Education

1857

Ringlets and ribbons flew
as the sisters skipped
past greengrocers' dazzling apples

until their mother finally called them in
to recite Shakespeare, model a clay head,
practice piano forte scales.

She insisted their fingers
be trained to the grip
of a brush,
to offer painted gifts

on their father's name day.
First indoor attempts:
small watercolors of sheep,
with girlish bursts
of cobalt and cerulean sky.

Berthe, the youngest, rushed
from the atelier
shocking their teachers

as she quickly began to sketch
grasses gathered
in bunches by the wind.
Let them stop me, she thought.

Who could keep up?
As if they were chasing a kite.

The Cottage at La Chaumière

1862

Papa Corot took her and Edma
to paint in the forests
at the River Oise and Fontainebleau,
the Chaumière in Normandy,

where Berthe copied his cottage,
thatched in hushed fairytale green
that would gradually lighten
beside the supple birch
she thought of as her tree.

He was more patient with Edma,
who did what he asked,
accepted his fatherly critiques
through whorls of pipe smoke,
exchanged her copies for his.

He scolded Berthe.
Once she forgot to paint
a step in the marble staircase
of her Italian study.
He demanded she paint it over.

She threw it out
with most of her early copies.
Pissarro saved
A View of Tivoli.

Daily Walk in the Quarter

Down the Rue Franklin in her black skirt
and white blouse, splattered with ochre,
black hair pulled back, deep black eyes,

Berthe lugs her satchel
laden with pigment tubes, sketchbooks,
tools of her work.

To a man on the street she looks odd
but full of purpose, a stark
Parisian sight, striding past

other women, weighed down
by baskets of legumes,
on the way to set up her easel

in the Bois du Boulogne,
her brushes determined arrows.
Where will they take her?

As she stabs her palette she mutters
shadow and angle,
swan, saw grass, chestnut tree.

Cross with unfinished sketches,
she's been known to toss them in the lake
and watch them float with lilies.

Berthe Morisot with a Fan

—Edouard Manet, 1872

It's a game between us,
my face half-hidden, only my lips

visible, my pink shoes peeking
below the hem of my obsidian cloud

of a dress. *Maman* keeps her eye on us,
embroidering in a corner of your studio.

I met you in the Louvre's second floor gallery,
when Fantin-Latour introduced us

as I was copying Rubens, a favorite master.
I was younger, still looked like a teachable

girl, but did not become your pupil.
You nudged me to keep working.

Later I learned you wrote Fantin
"what a shame" I wasn't a man.

Yes, I sign my works *Berthe Morisot*,
take no monsieur's *nom de plume*.

Even as you paint me we are colleagues.
A brush weighs the same

in our hands; a pair of industrious
demons, we meet eye to eye.

Our palettes thrive on tension.
Yours says black, mine white.

After I marry your brother Eugène
I never sit for you again.

The Harbor at Lorient

1869

The figure is not the first thing
the eye lands on, rather rooftops,
sky, masts, black hulls
like shoes lined up, along with
the feeling of being funneled,
as though you were about to be swept
out to sea in a sudden reversal,
where people have drowned
when the tide rushes back. Later

try to remember if someone
was sitting, a woman in white
with a cream-colored parasol
set against a solid wall.
Not a portrait, a pastoral, the figure
so far off to the right
the silvery reflection is there and not,
but how could that happen?
With water so flat, an afterthought of stillness,
you could have confused the white dress with clouds.

The Militia Billeted in the Studio

"Paris is on fire! . . . Throughout the day the wind kept blowing in charred papers; some of them still legible, have been carried here all day long. A vast column of smoke covered Paris, and at night, a luminous red cloud, horrible to behold, made it all look like a volcanic eruption!"

—Marie Cornélie Morisot, in a
letter during the Siege of Paris, 1870

Suspenders, boots, and swords akimbo all over the tiles, no place to work, Berthe's hands idle, her tools pushed in the corner, scaffold for spiders. How important it had been to capture the planes of the tea table, to choose this milky glass vase or that, arrange a gypsy scarf, cut blue hydrangeas now seeming like such trifles.

Unsafe to leave the house, unless absolutely necessary. In such close quarters she held her tongue over politics, wanted to be out of her parents' house, but felt it best to stay. Papa became obsessed with moving furniture around, saving the armoire, the mirror and console, all worthless to Berthe, who scolded him, in their father-daughter tug-of-war. He was determined to rescue these gargantuan walnut First Empire pieces, helpless to bring his family back together, to see his son Tiburce released from jail in Germany or fetch his other married daughters just hours by train from Paris.

Maman spent the war fretting over Berthe's lack of appetite. One afternoon at the table, trembling, Berthe took a bite of beef stew, then forgetting to put the spoon to her lips again, she fainted. Touching Berthe's gaunt cheekbones, her mother declared her consumptive.

That night Berthe dreamed the whole bloody terror, from beginning to end, the wounded in the Rue des Capucines, beheaded statues bumping down cobbles to the Seine. Her body shaking, she woke oddly calm. In the background, cannons, muffled, as if in cotton, the richochet of bullets on gray stone becoming a sound common as barking dogs. She was no longer startled when the windows shook, as if her dented dream bore the brunt of war, absorbed it, the dream became inoculation; it was all laid out, she would not be surprised. Having dreamed it, she it did not have to live it.

Now she wakes every day at a distance, protected from the fighting, writes to Edma: "Kisses for Bibi and Bijou. Papa continues to be in good health and is driving us all crazy."

Fédéric Bazille

"Do you know that all of our acquaintances have come out of the war without a scratch, except for that poor Bazille . . ."

—*Berthe Morisot to her sister, Edma, 1870*

The "tall fellow," as she thought of him,
his *View of the Village* not quite a portrait,
his genius to seat the tranquil girl
beneath the tree, her pink sash,
the houses on the hill
where he meant the eye to land:
an odd, new twist of perspective—yes,
it spoke to her.
She had to try it herself,
The Harbor at Lorient, her turning point.

Twenty eight, Berthe's age.
Big Bazille abandoned his oils
of family on the terrace,
muscular young men
on ropes swinging out over the water,
his life, one long summer afternoon.

He donned the uniform of the Zouave:
dramatic dark blue jacket,
white shirt, red balloon pants.

Towering over fellow recruits
he raised his bayonet
and jumped up in the first attack,
rushing over snow toward the Prussians,
as if to save the bullets
time and trouble;
the enemy's easy aim at his head
under the freezing plane trees
in *Beaune-La-Rolande*, November.

Correspondence

LES *PNEUMATIQUES*

Les petits bleus shoot across Paris via *pneumatique,* expediting contracts and invitations between arrondissements: admonitions and acceptances, auctions, Berthe's declarations and complaints hissing through tubes, a flurry of *billets doux,* exhibition announcements— " . . . one always derives benefit from exhibiting one's work, however mediocre it may be." reviews, tax payments, invoices, rsvp's, only the most important words between lovers, a cheerful closing, an endearment, *amicalement,* the outcries and polite regrets. The dear addresses: Ma chère fille, mon père, Madame, Monsieur. Kind Sir. Reckonings. Apologies.

STATIONERY

Blue paper folded, sealed with wax, unfolded, tucked
inside a blouse, their mother Marie Cornélie at her writing table in
    the corner,
her dignified signature polished with a flourish of her wrist, her
fountain pen,
bottles of blue and black ink, her letters blotted, her careful
    calligraphy,
Rue Franklin, Passy, my dears, outbursts of affection, the bises,
the double kisses, embraces and a sensible mother's advice.

MME. PONTILLON

1869, Edma, now married, writes her first letter to Berthe from Lorient, Brittany. Almost thirty, the sisters have always lived together at the same address: "I have never in my life written to you, my dear Berthe . . . ." They put down on paper sisterly intimacies, bits of gossip, rushes of affection, how much they miss each other, growing up side by side across a room, a table, in the garden, on the stairs. In the hallways they had only to turn to each other, with a gesture, a raised eyebrow, speaking not a word.

During the War

The Prussians blow up
the telegraph lines, letters must be sent by balloon,
manned or unmanned, over enemy camps, flames
shooting out to power the gondolas,
blue postcards lifted and carried, with luck, by the wind
or by pigeon. Pigeons are also carried
by balloon, partway, then released,
notes folded into tiny silver bands wrapped around bird leg bones.
Damp dead letters pile up in baskets at the post office.

Stamps in France

Timbres: decades of the goddess Ceres, deity of grapes, a sheaf of
wheat wound in her hair, represent liberty, the republic, replaced
by the Napoleons I, II, III, alternating: goddess goddess emperor
emperor emperor goddess goddess, blue, purple, green, purple, blue
the stamps stamped, the black ink never fades.

At Saint-Jean-de-Luz

1872

The sea of the Midi burns
all blue, a hue I hate;
a blaze, or some days the waves
lap lead gray, somber as mourning silk.
After breakfast my paintbrush,
more of a hammer,
weighs down my hand.
No purchase, as if on a cliff,
my mind can't catch.

The sails at standstill. Noon.
Clouds cross, cast a shadow,
leave me too distracted to paint
among the plane trees
and dry scorched earth of the south.

Edma stays out of the sun
with her new baby,
no more moments to explore
depths of aureolin or viridian,
bored, she tells me, crushed to think
what she has left behind.
We both read of Emma Bovary's routine days.

Playing *cache-cache*
with the baby in the early mornings
I yearn for what my sister has
yet wish she could place
her easel next to mine again.

Since she is not looking
at the sea the way I am
I hesitate to ask what she thinks of the light,
if it's breakable white glass or quick-change,
as wind shakes the cypress.

The Cradle

1872

I wanted the sleep she slept, the sleep
of Blanche, substantial baby, wide head
on the pillow, under the netting,
encompassed in the silence
of white tulle and voile.
I followed the line of silk
between mother and child cocooned in the stillness
of an afternoon, the whole fractious city
beyond closed curtains shot with rose.
Edma kept her thoughts to herself
while I worked; her fingers twined in the cradle's pale pink
netting, kept the world at bay, delicate, private,
steeped in the intimacy of drawn breath—
its own presence in the quiet of the infant's room.

Questions for Mr. Darwin

"I am reading Darwin; it is scarcely reading for a woman,
even less for a girl . . . ."

—*Berthe Morisot, from a letter, 1874*

The tortoise entered my dream last night
with his creeping gait . . . .

I read gentlemen ride them like horses.
Could I paint such a creature
or climb on its mud-green back?

With colored pencil I sketch
brown sparrows on my front step,
a caged blue parrot, my yellow lovebirds.

Could I sit beside you, Mr. Darwin, with my aquarelles,
steal from your scientist's eye,
as you draw, in black ink, your trembling finches,

a multitude of beaks, feathers, wings
across the page in a line
so subtle I can't identify the changes.

On Isabella Island, white sea birds
pant in the noon heat—I see their tongues—
and in the shallows around the boulders

coral spreads its alizarin crimson fan
like the sun rising underwater.
Could its rays touch

our Paris grays
in a world turned upside down?

The Wedding Ring

1874

Tête-à-Tête

Maman does not discourage me
from pursuing this métier until
one afternoon in the drawing room,
her arm sweeps toward my canvases.
She tells me she has
"no confidence in my talent . . ."
to think I could paint well enough
to give up a suitable union! Never! For this . . . .

At Fécamp

July, a sojourn with our families,
Eugène and I at our easels
on the cliff, near the old navy works.
We have to watch our step
down to the narrow beach to sketch
two boats being built,
sturdy ribs and scaffolding,
while the wind carries away our words
of endearment—though not all.
By supper I am betrothed
to my "honest and excellent young man."

The Registry

Our marriage begins in the cold, December,
gold bands on our stiff fingers, no guests,
I in gray linen, already feeling old
at thirty-three, shivering, as we leave the mairie.
Before the ceremony, signing the registry,
you write "man of property," and I,
"no profession."

But marriage, I see, can lift us
out from under
the shadow of a chaperone.
The ring on the carousel!
Wife, mother, painter.

Eugène Sits for a Painting

What does she see in me?
Shoulders, straw hat
by the window,
the sea at my back,

her dark eye at work
fixed on me but she
is elsewhere, glancing up
to scrutinize, then away.

There are rules.
Don't talk. Don't shift.
The world is focused on
her need to concentrate.

If Julie is here we play
a father-daughter game,
a dancing code with our fingertips,
make a wish and twine our pinkies

out of sight,
a tiny tattoo on our skin,
church and steeple,
cat's cradle without the string.

II

"This woman who seemed all her life to have painted for her own pleasure, as if art were no more than a pleasant distraction, had in fact pursued with passion, tenacity, and clear-sightedness an adventure where ease was only a mask and charm concealed rigor and strength, so that when she appeared to have done no more than brush the surface of the canvas, she had nevertheless gone beyond and dissolved appearances and miraculously enriched our vision."

—*Jean-Dominique Rey*

Stéphane Mallarmé

In letters he asked after the greyhound, Laertes,
his gift to Julie, calling the slender hound
the "sole defender" in a household
of women, asking if Laertes
liked the sea, and to please remember him
". . . to good Laertes, as Hamlet called him."

Symbolist friend, congenial genius,
he shared Berthe's fascination
with fashion and houses, became Julie's
guardian, and liked to jot down
quick quatrains when invited to

Berthe's Thursday dinners, or, if he invited them
to his Tuesday gentlemen's soirees:

"Their diligent greyhound
Will deliver this letter
To the Ladies Manet at Roche Place,
Portrieux, Côtes-du-Nord." by *pneumatique*

If the only ladies . . . should she and Julie
hide . . . wear trousers?
Most at ease seated and daydreaming,
Mallarmé let Berthe coax him into taking
walks under the beech trees
at Fontainebleau, an immense and gentle canopy
like a dance hall, a splendid place
for his daughter's wedding.

In a postcard scrawl from the train
he thought he saw the windows
of the Manets' new villa, Le Mesnil,
shutters thrown back, one stark
wisteria vine like a pencil line
winding over the stucco.

The poet will write his preface
to the catalog for her
posthumous exhibition:
six celebrated paragraphs
impenetrable as his poems,
a tribute to his *friendly Medusa* . . . .

The Abandoned Book

1886

Mallarmé has told us he will
create a book to be opened
    from any angle and read
like a poem we can enter
    from any line, a painting we can turn
upside down, see the image as if reflected,
    examined from any distance,
a volume to be called

    The Lacquered Drawer,
  each artist-friend assigned
    a poem of his to illustrate.
  His lines leave us flabbergasted,
    bouleversé. Not hurt,
    he is puzzled that we
can't grasp his verses'clarity.

Mine is "White Waterlily,"
  depart with it; steal silently away,
rowing, little by little . . .
  I make a study, *arbres roux:*
my tree trunks in the Bois de Boulogne
  thin as waterlily stems
   disappear in the lake
   as if viewed through the surface,
my first rough try at a drypoint.

I am pleased to hear it was admired
by Monet, who knows to look at the world
   as though it were a watery
mirror, never the real,
   waterlily mad like all of us,
giving in to an urge for floating
   pointed petals offered up.

A reader will not locate the book
   on any shelf.
Only Renoir completes his work,
   an etching, *Woman of Yesteryear,*
   the other pages lost
    adrift in history,
our dear Mallarmé's idea barely under way . . .

He can't help it if we
   set down our brushes,
our pictures half-rendered.
   He counts on our smiles.
"The ideal flower in a bouquet,"
he says, "is always
   the one that's missing."

Julie

Berthe taught Julie to read
from her watercolor alphabet.
They shared Christmas crayons,
packed sketch pads and pastels
for excursions to the Tuileries
where Julie knelt on a low bench,
to watch the marionettes
or sat, her back straight in a rowboat,

Afternoons they climbed to Montmartre,
counting the steps
up to blinding white Sacré Coeur.
Tea on the terrace with Renoir and Aline, the friendliest
house in Paris, despite his scant artist resources,
cracked teapot on a threadbare cloth.

Aline wore no ring of his, scandalous
to some Parisians, but not to Berthe.
What mother was happier
hugging little Pierre
before she let him go
to race with Julie at the foot of the garden.

Renoir painted Julie at ten, round face,
hair cut close to her ears, and again,
curled tresses brushing
her shoulder, at sixteen.
And he asked to paint them both,
mother sideways, silver-haired,
daughter, in beribboned hat,
meeting his gaze.

She challenged herself
with an outsize canvas, painted
again and again an A-shaped ladder

leaning in the cherry tree, Julie
on the highest rung, almost lost
in a tangled braid of green,
her cousin raising the basket of summer fruit.

With Eugène gone, in grief,
they drew even closer.
Berthe knew her daughter
would grow up to be an artist herself.
In the garden, sitting down to paint, Julie saw
"pink in the light, violet in the shadows."

Self-Portrait

1885

Who are you?
A riddle you ask us to solve.
You were on your way
out the door and we called you back.
What urgency drives you?
Your black eyes bear down,
your mouth open as if
you were still speaking.
Wiry gray escapes from dark curls,
shoulders in plain brown taffeta,
your only finery a charcoal bow
tied tight at your neck.
That's where you end.
You are old
and won't grow much older.

Your friend De Régnier declares
your bearing "military and abrupt."
So be it. You nurture the salute inside you,
can't be bothered with niceties,
brusque, never satisfied
with your work or yourself,
you fling back the door,
tell us, quick, take a look
at the mess of your studio,
turn to rinse out a brush
while we stare, shrug off our praise.

Young Girl Reading

1888

To go into oneself and close the door of the cage.

To make oneself into a small bird
in a cage not singing but silent.

To be lost in thought in the heat of the conservatory
ordinary sun beating on the glass,
to feel the brushstrokes' action.

By staying quiet one appears obedient.

To be at the center of unruly brushstrokes,
one feather among
wild frenzied feathers scratchy on the canvas,

caught in a maelstrom
orange, red, green cacophony.

Oil that at first resembles
pastel or colored pencil,
brushstrokes like feathers in a whirlwind.

To turn the pages, one after the other,
to feel the ruffled pages lift their wings.
To be quiet when the bird inside is not.

Miss Cassatt and Mlle. Morisot

1886

Did the critics misinterpret Berthe's "wanting
to capture something that passes . . .
just something, the least of things . . . ?"

In 1874 at the auction, an oil of hers,
Interior, fetched the most, followed by
On the Grass, a pastel,

though in the boisterous crowd Renoir
swore he overheard
a muttered, "shameless hussy,"

as Berthe stepped past.
Mary Cassatt's canvases
were hung beside hers, one

always preferred over the other.
Couldn't reviewers see
Berthe used color, Mary a deep

black line to create form?
Berthe called on Mary
on Sundays, at Marly-le-Roi,

pausing in the hallway
to compose herself
at the vexing mirror.

They painted worlds
they woke to, flow of zinc-white
drapes beside a branch

of blue hydrangeas,
children in a realm of rosy fists,
but a treacherous eye

gave it away, landed
like a wasp, its stinger digging:
Choose. Compare.

Mary's oeuvres were declared
complete, Berthe's slashing
brushstrokes puzzled,

as a floating image
disappeared, unfinished
at the edges.

The Hydrangea or Two Sisters

1894

Berthe has to stash her brushes
in the kitchen cupboard
when someone comes to call,
but her implements are always at the edge
of her mind, the corner of her eye.
Pendulum, minute hand,
tick of the mantel clock, gong
of the grandfather in the hall.
Time, a reminder, running
away with its bells,
its little ticks and tocks,
its gears, plays tricks.
Only a few steps
from corridor to kitchen,
she is out of breath,
impatient, as the pendulum
swings back,
to be alone again.

It's easy to miss
the skein of yarn, poppy red,
set down in one sister's lap,
(her hands needed to adjust her sister's hair)
a few rows along the knitting needle,
fixed like the hour hand of the clock.

Berthe tackles the late afternoon
indoor light, borrowing from her friend,
Renoir, his delineation, the way
he uses blues.
She contrasts a stealthy shade

against the girls' pale skin and blouses,
the skin of girls who stay indoors.
One fixes the other's hair,
clips a hydrangea behind her ear.
The sisters chat,
as Berthe and Edma used to.

Someone calls to them.
They are in no hurry,
dawdlers, late risers, not sure
if they are going out or staying in,
or who might come to call
at 40 Rue Villejust.

Portrait of Berthe Morisot

—painted by her sister Edma Pontillion, 1865

She doesn't recognize herself.
She'd never felt as calm,
as full of purpose as Edma made her look
on this canvas years ago, the way she clutches
the brushes, her aura softened by velvet browns,
the dancing gold earring, red blouse,
like details in a painting by an old master,
an allegory, but of what?

She, Edma and Yves, a trio,
close as little girls,
determined to figure out the rules,
not always following them,
reveled in running, ringlets flying,

too tired now,
to travel to each other,
their hair too white, their legs
stabbed by shooting pains.
Moving in different circles
of distance, obligations,
they rarely see each other.

Sometimes she thinks she hears
Edma and Yves,
heels on the oak floor,
laughter spiraling up the stairs
in the Rue Franklin,

Tiburce in his sailor suit
holding the toy boat
he smashed in the Tuileries.
She remembers their Mother
having to rein them in.

How would *Maman* feel now
knowing her children no longer speak
unless they have to,
have fallen out,
too late, Yves laments,
to bring warmth
to the "real wall of ice"
between them.

Conversations with Eugène

Had she ever wondered what he was thinking
while she painted him?

One of her faults, he told her,
"You're never willing to praise
my own canvases."
He managed her sales and exhibits.
She called him her best friend, counselor,
tended to him while they moved
from Paris to Mézy, in search of
houses without damp as he slowly
faded from her.

His last months, feverish, his mind whirled
with thoughts of repairs, their new chateau,
Le Mesnil, its cracked black shutters, draughty salon,
and broken red roof tiles.
Each step she took on the stairs,
dusty with plaster, evoked his illness.
Without him she couldn't live
in the weak light of these rooms,
recalling their days at the seaside
where she had to cajole him to pose for her.

He died and she thought she wanted to die too,
but no, the truth was, she wanted to be younger.
For strength she read Montaigne,
jotted down thoughts in her journal.

"My Thonjoun! My lamb," he would whisper,
his inflection difficult to call up now,
to hear his raspy voice again–
if just to have him accuse her once more,
  "Yours is only the surface of a heart."

Was it true?

Distracted, driven, all those years, she had guarded
her time in the studio.
This morning she cursed her own "overblown ambition."
What kind of wife had she been?
It was too late to ask him.

Now a "small sea channel"
separated them, as if she were "Dover and he
Calais," so close, but they could not hold hands,
the chasm between them grown too wide to share
a single thought.

Girl with Greyhound

1893

Re-reading her mother's letters
Julie bursts into tears, wishes she had been
a better daughter . . . thankful

her mother left her this painting, her most important gift,
though in it she wears
black, her eyes are puffed and purple
in mourning for Papa.

The pale blue velvet armchair is
left empty for him, but the chair
could also be waiting for M. Mallarmé,
Oncle Parrain, or Maman herself.

On the wall, the Japanese print that greeted her
every morning, so often
she stopped looking:
a man kneeling, in green.
She wondered who he was
in faraway Kyoto.
She always meant to ask.

At her knee, on the flowered carpet
beside the sofa where her mother
plumped up cushions and set out on the table
the little box for calling cards,

her tawny Laertes,
four-footed, sure-footed friend,
coat of wheat like her own head of hair,
ready to spring up
and race with her outside
through the waist-high grass.

Last Work: *The Little Marcelle*

1895

At the posthumous exhibit,
The Little Marcelle

painted while Julie thrashed
hot under the white duvet
then plunged deep

into shivers, as if being rolled in snow,
too weak to climb the stairs and watch her
mother make short purple brushstrokes
on this unfinished portrait;

do-si-do of sickness
in the house,
round of contagion,
daughter wheezing

harsh whistling breaths,
as mother set her brush down,
pressed a cold compress
to her daughter's flushed forehead

set down her brush
and caught her breath,
her death.

In the frame
that sad child's eyes peered
straight into fever.

"'We All Die With Our Secret.'"

— Berthe Morisot in her journal, 1895

The Harbor at Lorient, Hide and Seek,
View of Paris from the Trocadaro,
saying the names of my paintings
helps me to sleep . . .

Mother, daughter, wife,
I lay down my weapon, my palette,

the secret self I've lived with
slowly drained of color
like ashes from a love note
crushed in my locket.

Give me a moment
in my favorite morning light at Bougival,
opening the shutters in the house at Le Mesnil,

what they tell me I was best at, painting
just after waking, dew on the grass, the hours stretching ahead.

Or something shade and color can't give shape to,
just out of reach, a sound beyond earshot, footsteps disappearing
down a corridor in the house on the Rue Franklin.

Whose hands are those on the worn piano keys
picking out a pianissimo, the notes floating
around the corner, gone?

Somewhere I wanted to go something I wanted
to do something I did or did not do
expires as I do this afternoon;

my disappointments closing up
lose their splendid magenta
like the weeks-old amaryllis on the windowsill.

Julie, hurry, a whisper
about the day, the very day . . . .

An Art of Absence

1895

What she left out:
a ruthless black
boredom,
bitter self-critique,
an *irritated melancholy*
her second nature;
loneliness and war.

On her death certificate
as on her certificate of marriage:
"No profession."

Almost overnight
caring for her daughter
she succumbed.

Her last letter to Julie:
"Give some souvenir of me to Aunt Edma and to your cousins;
to your cousin Gabriel, Monet's *Boats Under Repair.* . .
Give something to the two concierges.
Don't cry. . . ."

The Mozart Sonata

1894

A Saturday morning
duet for cousins,
faces blurred,
fingers, chin, elbow,
violin and piano.
Above the keys
green stalks rise in a blue vase,
curled petals falling.
The bow hesitates,
hands stumble
over the same notes
as sunlight sifts through
pearl curtains,
the air stirred in disarray.
Practice is over.

Musée Marmottan Monet
An American woman and her mother visit today

2016

What do they look like?
daughter, mother, both old
as they enter the museum,
in this duke's former hunting lodge
in Passy, near the Bois du Boulogne,
where Berthe spent her life.
Their hands on the curved bannister,
they have left Monet in the basement,
climbed the marble stairs to Morisot

to see watercolors of daughters,
pastels of hair being brushed, the soft, safe world
of ladies at the cheval glass,
the coveted white dress,
that dips at the back,
afternoons at dressing tables
to make oneself look pretty
for someone else's wedding or garden party.

In gilt-edged mirrors,
they glimpse their own aging faces;
quickly turn their heads away
can't believe what they see,
the echoing image,
the years that don't halt for them.

Around the corner they expect
the artist herself
as though they had known her.

Inside them the ghosts are stalled:
ghosts that were storming
out of dressing rooms,
coveting almost the same white gown.

Glass cases in the dim corridor are filled with more—
watercolors, sketches, so many of Berthe's
descendants continuing art,
early sepia photos, faded letters,
holding the history of her circle,
painters and poets,
intertwined by friendship, marriage,
a mesmerizing kinship difficult to track.

Windows open onto a garden
mother and daughter imagine
they can step into,
re-joining children with butterfly nets
and ladders propped in the trees,
thick grass at Bougival,
views they want to appropriate,

of a world Berthe
was trying to capture she knew
even then was disappearing
among smokestacks
and barges on the estuary.

A world they never lived in,
mother and daughter,
though they yearn for it as if they had.

Fragile and frayed by day's end,
their heads cocooned in dusk,
in color and texture of the late last century,
they worry they can't complete
the few blocks' walk to the bus stop
through streets thick with exhaust.

Guards close the heavy 19th century doors,
locks turn, one after the other.
Late light, light
she might have liked,
filters in the dust motes.

GHOST
PEACE

Arriving at Bradford Point

Walking among scattered apples,
I had to watch my feet,
easy to trip and twist an ankle
distracted by the scent of ripening.
Tall grass wound up the rungs
of a ladder leaning in a crooked tree.

The cottage sat akimbo on the lawn,
old henhouse with a room
to sleep in, not logically situated,
at an odd angle to the road.
Which yard did it belong in?
I couldn't tell.

I sat down on the couch, my eyes
at sea level followed the line
to the water, the perfect range;
everything around me loose
and knocking, aching but tethered,
anchored or knotted, at some point assured
nothing would float away, not even me, my body
trying to carve out its perch.

Backstop in the Woods

I'd have to find somebody
who played there as a child,
threw a ball to the squatting catcher,
slid into home base, skinned a knee, whose house
was nearby—used to take a short cut

from his cul-de-sac. He could lead me
through a privet hedge grown wild
a little way into the woods
where the trees are too sparse
to get lost in.

Old oak leaves were left to pile up,
the space that was the field
lost in scrub. An apple tree or two
blocked the way,

the chain link still upright, sturdy enough
for a younger sibling to climb
or rattle with both hands.

Years later I passed this backstop, lost
in thought, walking in a group single file.
I tried to double back
but it was late and others called.

Urgencies and Contingencies

Are there to-do lists
in the afterlife?

Requirements, not for entering, but once
eternal time begins or the concept of a day
ends.

Permission granted to use an external wristwatch?
A Swiss one. The thin gold band admired.

Appointments to keep
or let slip, admonitions to self
not to oversleep.

Reach for a pen a dream voice says
and write this down.

Something urges me forward
won't let me sit still.

All my life I was called away
to cover a desk.
I don't know if I will find one here.

Or clues as to what will be urgent.
Waiting to be assigned to a specific quadrant.
Not urgent and not important.

In heaven have they heard
of the concept of structure?

As in, how to structure
your eternal time.

I keep looking at my wrist
but my watch is gone,
and I feel completely naked.

Off the Old Post Road

1.

This summer of abundance
hummingbirds swirl
between my feeder
and the one next door,
more than in any recent year.

I have to keep boiling
sugar water,
let it cool, before filling
the swaying crimson feeder.

2.

Not much room
between townhouses,
six feet of deck,

railing that needs paint,
obscured by scrawny cedars,
sprawling sand cherry.

Tinny chirp at dawn: on the other side
of the ragged cloak of leaves,
not a bird but a car door opener.
The cars back out

of their numbered parking spaces
slowly turn, smooth sound
of tires on pavement;
in the evening, their return.

3.

Sometimes at dusk my neighbor
sings in Portuguese
as he strums his guitar.

I can't understand a word
yet his song feels private,
wrong of me to overhear.

He sings as if he is not
a deck away, half hidden
by unraveling river birch,
rather near mountains or the sea.

His voice makes me a shy
sunset eavesdropper,
not meant myself
to be transported.

Coming up the walk the day before,
we chatted, pleasantries.
I asked him,
beija flor, he said,
the Portuguese for hummingbird.

Contemplations

She drove home in the dark in a downpour.
He bowed his head before an open window.
The calendar was kept beside the bed, all its pages blank.
The casement windows were thrown back
against the shutters for fresh air.
She pulled the shade down inside herself.
It grew darker as if before a gathering storm.
He said one day follows like any other.
The afternoon was often a lost cause.

She remembers a photograph of the awnings on her
 grandmother's house.
Despite the awnings, the heavy velvet furniture was hot.
She is forgetting to get up off her couch.
Even in summer on a rainy day
there is a darkness she has not seen before.
She forgets to look outside herself.
It is as though she forgets the outside is there.
She must remember to close the window or the rain pours in
 on the sills,
to leave the keys to the house somewhere she can find them herself.

He asks her if her rear view mirror is always this dark;
odd she has never noticed.
Cocooned in herself,
maybe she has grown used to the darkness,
unaware there is another option.
Crickets. Frogs or peepers? She's not sure what she is hearing.
The air is close and still, makes it difficult to breathe.
They disagree on whether they have seen a fisher.
Rain, often predicted, fails to materialize.

Trying to identify a tree:
Leaves like those of a locust appear lined up in a derelict wind.
Pale green outer shell with faint scent of citrus.
Picture in tree book, decide: hickory?
Determine if oak, ash, birch, or beech.
Able to break off and examine a branch from another tree,
not locust, rule out hickory, established: in walnut family.
Walnut family, dark 19th century furniture, valuable and
    sought after
for a sideboard, a birthing bed passed down, or a judge's desk.
Black walnut, hard to crack open, even with a gavel,
and when you do you inhale a grassy, floral smell.
The wind leaves a bitter aftertaste.

She spotted a baby rabbit hiding in the boxwood beside
    the front door.
The most vulnerable of animals. Why don't they run?
Calmer than squirrels and chipmunks.
They twitch, nibble, contemplate, then take their time,
slowly hop away across the grass, showing their white tails.
Were those its cries she heard at 3 in the morning, getting
    torn apart?

She lived in a house once with a rabbit allowed to roam free.
Someone had principle, took a stand against cages,
but who followed the rabbit and cleaned up after him?
What happened to him, the young man who disapproved of cages?
Last week she found a skeleton stretched out beside the oak,
picked clean, save for one perfect white fur paw.

She looks down at her life in miniature,
like the layout of Beijing in the museum she wanted to visit,
and moves herself around,
sees herself strolling through the hutongs,
crouching down to peer into lives
she has no business examining.

The Imperial Palace, the exhausting lengths to cover.
She prefers silence when she walks
yet feels trapped in a vise of her own thoughts.

She asks for a ruler. She wants the measurement exact.
She makes herself smaller, maybe memory
shrinks things, feelings, until they can be gripped
in her palm, her fist.
Are they clay, snow, or stone?

Some memories are like the floaters the eye doctor tells her
will never go away; she'll just get used to them.
Flotsam, jetsam. In the end these may be
her only possessions.

Orchard Lane

She has walked by it often
and when invited in
forgets her manners,
makes herself at home.
She knows a house like it

but this front door is wider,
the blue and braided rug
at the top of the stairs
laid on hardwood,
the ceiling higher.

The bannister her hand knew
on the left now curves to the right.
She steps back, as though caught
in the mirror in a dream,
daily household tasks distorted,
stacks of folded laundry falling open,
a door not quite clicking shut.

In the yellow kitchen on a rise:
more sunlight, less clutter.
Calm for a moment,
she can take in
the remaining apple trees.

A block away her old house,
where her son grew up, still sits
in lowland, a mossy hollow,
winged bark euonymus
fiery red in the fall,
another face looking out
the kitchen window.

Sketches for Edward Hopper

1.

Now I am the age you were
when you began to paint in earnest.

Every day at work
I watch a view of yours:
brick wall, drawn shades

fire escape, sky
and moving cars
reflected in the panes.

Walking home yesterday:
empty tanneries,
man smoking on a public bench,

gas station beside a house
that seemed too tidy
for a family, its geraniums

too red like the lipstick
I imagined the woman inside
applying at the mirror.

The shoppers looked like me,
already in their forties,
not who they'd planned to be.

Later I went out again
to walk alone, as if
it were not dangerous.

I sat at a counter
in a coffee shop
my back to everyone

night alternating
with neon.

2.

A room nothing collects in,
no gloves, no clutter,
tells me, finally,
no one belongs here

and no one seems to talk,
even to herself.
The two young women
in the restaurant
don't seem to be talking.

But his ledgers bulge
with words, black urgent ink,
scrawled sketch of whatever
he was working on,
surrounded by fragments,
mostly his wife's
unadorned statements.

He won't tell his story.
He leaves that to us,
sparse living rooms,
solitude, not one dusty speck
of solicitude.

I thought I felt enough
at home in his paintings
to tease out a thread
yet his emptiness
elbows mine out of the way,
unspoken, hidden agenda.

His abyss and my abyss,
two stones to rub.

My mother has seen enough.
To her his images say
Ellensburg, Washington, 1933,
long car rides with her father
out to the hops farm.
Even the Manhattan blocks of color
evoke for her
the desolate West.

Hand on the forehead,
his or mine?
All the sentences it took,
sealed away, packed up in valises.
He didn't use words.
I need them.
When I glimpse his silences,
I have to look away.

Goldilocks

She wants someone to tell her
what kind of animal she is,

the name of the creature
that crawls inside another's shell,

that burrows and borrows,
spinning on foreign wings,

wandering, aimless, through an open gate,
stepping, mother may I, farther in …

picking up a snow globe, shaking it hard,
turning someone else's world

upside down. She has been here before, doubling
as the sour daughter, who leaves a trace,

damp pillowcase, twisted sheets,
breath evaporating on the spoon.

She needs to report whose bed
she has been sleeping in,

waking with a key in her hand,
no glass slipper, no mirror, no red hood;

these come later, the appointment made,
the proper door.

The Public Bride

Frothed in ivory, what language is she speaking?
She stalks through the park, trailed by a photographer
and an attendant in tight magenta, no groom in sight,
giving orders to the phone in her palm.
I think she's looking for a world to rule,
brushing the other brides aside among the willows.
She shows a sense of time, of timing matters.
She gets a leg up on the rail above the swan boats,
her six-inch candy apple heel shines, as she leans back
for the photograph. She out-swans the swans, their hiss.
We wouldn't want to get too close, yet should we
back away or be ready to throw up our hands
when she tosses the bouquet that matches,
the love-lies-bleeding, tear-your-heart-out-red?

A History of the English Tea Cup

For centuries tea was sipped
lukewarm in small cups
fragile as eggs
held in two hands.
The handle was added when tea
was to be served
still hot, a saucer placed beneath
the cup to hold the spoon
after the sugar dissolved
in a bergamot or jasmine steam.

Now you stir and stir
and recall the fun of an aunt
late Northwest afternoons,
peering in the almost empty cup
at shapes in the black leaves
she called your future:
a gate, a small boat.
You trusted
she knew every detail
and how those years would be
cheerfully delivered.
It was all in her hands,
tapered like your mother's
in the rainy dark.

Coin

There is always a thought needing to be expressed,
a note, a pale blue idea left on a pillow. Sometimes
I draw a blank, clouded by a lack of urgency, nowhere I need
to go, nowhere I need to be. I remember a mill
is a tenth of a cent but who will give me
a penny for my thoughts?
If I see a dime in the grass I leave it
for a child to pick up, good luck by proxy,
thinking of old phone booth days,
when, hungry, out of the rain,
hoping for a change of fortune,
I reversed the charges.

Please

It was a bit in the mouth, the metal braces,
a bite out of Eden, apples bitten into
thrown on the ground by wild children,
or a bittern witnessed on the strand in Belgium.
Bitte is one of the few words
she remembers, please, but it sounds like
bitter, a girl, curious about the bitters
on her father's shelf, scolded for keeping her
head down, tearing away at her skin,
not looking up and smiling
as expected.

Woodstock, Manson, and the Moon

The moon was in Aquarius.
She was not at Woodstock.
Manson walked up the driveway in L.A.
How many said they were at Woodstock
or on their way but the car broke down?
Bumper-to-bumper.
She was hitchhiking in Ireland,
walking from the main road miles
to seaside hostels.
How many miles to Galway?
How many miles to the moon?
How many people were part of the murders?
One small step. How much rocket fuel?
One giant leap.
Sharon Tate was pregnant.
Mother may I?
How many details she has forgotten
in her own life, yet she remembers this,
words scrawled on the wall.

The moon was in Manson.
The Manson in the moon.
She tried to read *Ulysses*,
lugged in her backpack,
her friends downstairs dancing.
She read the headlines easily.
Men walked on the moon.
Manson and the girls walked up the driveway
under his spell, his thumb.
Is a murder in a house domestic?
One Manson has just died in prison at 61:
she was married twice, she had a life in prison!
Ride a cock horse to Woodstock.
How many miles to the moon?

To Manson?
How many days in prison?
X's on the calendar. She heard the music.
Hendrix. Joplin. Cass.
How many music makers dead?
The Mansons left no widows.
The moon was in Aquarius.
Woodstock took no prisoners.

Vietnam blew up.
How many miles to the murders?
How many murders to the mile?
In black and white
they televised the moon landing.
One by one they'll die in prison.
A hard rain fell at Woodstock.
Mud churned in Ireland.
She had blisters on her feet.
She read the naked crowds were peaceful.
No one had seen anything like it.
The long-haired girls walked with him
along the jasmine-scented driveway . . . .

To the Tree Outside My Window

Ten years you've stood there,
ornamental.
I've looked through you.

Which of your branches made me
turn my head this morning
and delve into your names?

Sarvis or serviceberry,
sorbus out of Shakespeare,
saskatoonberry, juneberry,

birds and squirrels as if
in hidden pictures hunting
in your skinny branches.

Yet you are also shadblow
or shadbush for the fish
that swim upstream in April.

Your oval leaves signal,
so the story goes,
that now a country preacher

in the Blue Ridge
can travel thawed dirt roads
to speak at clapboard churches;

white blossoms torn
in a breeze mean the ground
is soft enough for burial.

I must often pass you in the woods,
unknowing, where one small tree
grows like any other,

not exclaimed over
like the scarlet winterberry
or massive pasture oak.

People have sown orchards,
inviting strangers on their land
to gather handfuls of your fruit

and in city parks they plant
groves to stroll or hurry past
or fall asleep under with a book.

The hummingbird feeder swings
on one of your branches in this tiny,
temporary Eden

while already your leaves
are yellow, soon to rust
against your silver bark,

your steady presence.
I have only to look again and you are
there, or not, never were.

At the End of the Day

"A lot of work is about waiting."

—*Philip Levine*

Wait at the time clock to punch out
the minute hand to move to 5
each clutching a time card as we
wait to punch
wait for the customer to approach
take his forms
wait for coffee, lunch
two lengths of time
push me pull me
wait it out
point A to Point B
time strung
like a clothesline
work, home, time off
voice on the phone
what are your hours
not enough in the day
first floor clock
never agrees with the second floor
their minute hands argue, tiny swords
they never join in a synchronized swim
agree to disagree
unless someone grabs keys,
taps her wristwatch
as she watches a colleague
button his coat
pull on each boot
someone rattles the front door
too late
wait for the elevator
to rise at glacial pace

the doors to open close
timer out of sync
pitch dark on the walk
activate the alarm
slam it off try again
turn back to test the outer door is locked

Maze

A voice out of the past
does not pull me back.
I am not starting where I left off,
clammy receiver in my hand,
my tone all business.
The voice evokes no tremors
no sadness.
The future is contained.
The future has a fence around it.

Why weren't you, a walker, interested in that maze? he asked,
a place for walking prayer, a place to sidestep a question
among the leafy alders, the shivering trees
on this small peninsula, the crumbling stone walls, the *allée*.
I don't know. I could start but wouldn't know where to stop.
Not a maze where you could get lost and never find your way out.
It had a special name. He was kind and gentle but
needling, admonished on almost every point, but quietly, politely.
That was his way, said discouraged rather than *prohibited*.
I broke off early, went home. My phone service had been cut off
suddenly, no warning, the bill not paid up, not that I expected a call
but I felt agitated and bereft. I liked to keep the lines open, in case,
the way a mystic waits, breathes in and out, for a special message,
even at my age in this day and age.

Statute of limitations.
The one on feelings has run out.
My old address book leaves me cold.
Those names crossed out
in anger, I can't decipher now
but I won't discard the book
bound with rubber bands,
its pages falling out.

Restless movers, my generation—
all over the country, at least we started out
that way, I'm rarely now on the West Coast.

I trace the same few miles
to work and back,
avoid the long commute,
Walk the same streets
in the shady enclave.
Safety in that.
I'm about to move again
three miles, in limbo,
floating free.

The limitations of the statute:
name, date and serial number.
An old roommate I failed
to recognize.
She had been blonde and vague,
with cotton candy hair.
Now she was stout and loud,
hair the same as everyone else's.
She was angry, not hurt,
her look confirmed
something she suspected about me, all along,
the commanding way she spoke
my whole name, first and last.

The day-old purple iris,
dark as a black eye,
left a stain on my fingers
like schoolgirl's ink.
Its floppy petals spilled out of the glass,
black liquid drip unstoppable,
an obstacle, an affront.

Does anyone know where I am?
No one has come looking for me.
This pause, crevice in a life
in which I'm inadvertently hiding,
not sure I want to be found.

Silhouette

Standing in the long high-ceilinged hallway
what is it I feel? That I should balance
on one leg? Absorb a ghost peace?

As children we were told
to crouch down under our desks,
to put our arms
over our heads or march into a corridor
with no windows, just the dark,
and the walls would protect us.

A cool empty passage
and a looking glass,
which tells me what?
That my hair is out of place,
that the world repeats itself over and over.

Hawthorne's Old Manse

The tour guide wants me to see
how one pane in the old glass was scratched
by a diamond ring, the author's wife's name,
Sophia, in watery script, still visible
after two hundred years, a detail
a visitor on her own might miss
but the only thing I remember
all these years after my father brought me here.

Dusk is rolling in on mist over the Concord River.
Now I stop listening.
My mind wanders past the velvet rope
up the stairs, forbidden to visitors . . . .

In one room a table is set as if for tea. Idly I think,
someone has to keep the cups
dusted, to straighten the lace tablecloth each day.
Someone has to keep up with history, keep it in its place,
although history, like the river, keeps shifting.
If I look twice, I see
the green wing chair in the corner,
where my father would have sat down to read.

1957

Mallarmé, synonym for obstacle
in their suburban saltbox, his poems
a wooden crate for her mother
to kick her way out of,
reciting his lines
as she vacuumed.

A classical *explication de texte*
of "An Afternoon of a Faun,"
the professor deemed
perfect but out of date.

Mallarméan. Sysiphisian.

His name, deceptive, mellifluous, a pillow
to float on, a cat's name;
Mallarmé, almost a palindrome,
a private family
symbol, a syndrome
demanding to be deconstructed,
with a stuttering undercurrent.

A river the opposite of Lethe
kept her mother awake,
churning hot and molten.

Her mother let the needle drop,
seconds of scratching:
Debussy in a minor key.
The child held the large cardboard
sleeve, listened, stared

at the drawing of a faun
without a w, not a young deer,
but a man, of sorts,
with no shirt on,
his hooves disturbing the hardwood.

A flute wound through the glade
of the living room.
Violins, pan pipes, a harp.
She sat and swung her legs,
not knowing, not wanting
to be asked
what she was hearing.

Under the Surface

In the middle of a province,
she hears a language she almost knows,
words thrown out at her idly like pebbles.

She sits on a hillside in an old amphitheater,
sage grows out of the warm stones. Bees
idle in the olive trees. Nearby a stone cottage,
its door opening to dark, smells of rot, holds a buzzing nest.

She leaves herself in the underbrush.

All the lovely places she spent summers,
the northern island, icy water, steps down
to a dock at low tide,
the turquoise pools. Two and two together,
a mother and father somewhere,
her screams unheard, her head pushed down
in rust-colored waves. She kicks and pedals,
tries to translate into up for air.

The Cooling Pavement

The hawk in the road guarded his carcass.
We waited for him to swivel his neck,
to train his eye on us. Come on. Come on.

I couldn't look at her
at work he said
the way she voted.

If we'd approached would he have cocked his mottled head
or attacked? Would he have thought we came for the
crushed black wings and claws smashed at his feet?
Minutes passed elastic with feathers and blood.

The office
wasn't big enough.
I kept my back
to her.

He had the road to himself.
We drove closer, waiting for his eye to blink.

The Visit

The first thing you ask for is a map
but they won't give you one.
The road out here has a number,
a star route, and each sparse house
a p.o. box. The neighbors are told
not to stare. You took a bus from a named city
to get to this stop, a crossroads with a number on the plains
at the edge of a mountain range, then climbed aboard
an old school bus, gray painted over yellow.

A visitor, like you, gives up
his license, his car keys, money,
and you are given a number
like a star route yourself, a latitude
and a longitude and twenty minutes
to sit in a locked room
and talk. They don't want you to know
where you are, as if you were blindfolded
and spun around, without the blindfold,
with no point of reference,
no point of origin, or destination.

They won't tell you the name of this corridor,
the entranceway you are standing in,
waiting in one gated box within another box,
as keys clang, wheels spin within locks,
the tumblers turn through their stages.

The one you visit doesn't know
how to describe where his cell is.
They don't want you to know either.
A window up high, 4 by 4 inches,
like a truck's rear view mirror, reveals
a wash of gray or, on lucky days, robin's egg blue,
no object, no movement, not even a bird's wing.
Can you almost pretend to read the clouds?

He is allowed thirty minutes a day
outside in a recessed well, angled
so deep he can't see over the lip.
Maybe, raising his head like a horse
he can smell the licorice scent of sagebrush.

The clock is ticking.
You and he sit on either side of the table.
Off-kilter yourself, you have brought him
what you can, a skein of color
(even the TV is black-and-white)
and the fleeting exchange of names.

He knows the mountains are out there.
The mountains have turned into questions:
Could he see them once? Could he name them?
Colorado a state of what? The names used to
mean something. Now they are reduced to syllables.
He is forgetting his capitals,
how to point left or right.
No compass. Even if he knew true north
and could head in that direction,
he would hit a wall, where would he go?
The syllables are fading like a page left
too long in the sun
he has to strain his eyes to see.
Prairie dog, tumbleweed, plateau,
what they taught him in geography.

This land could be called beautiful or desolate
if he could choose the one word he was looking for,
the adjective to explain
what they deprive him of, what the thick manual says
to withhold, what they will deprive you of, too.
The few things left he can count
on his fingers, a sense of the senses,
key, lock, steel door
being slammed, every sound memorized
and cherished, eight footsteps
coming for him.

In a Garden Cemetery

Along
>borders of
>>cobblestone,
>>>deep in
>even,
>>fresh
>>>grass
hydrangeas are

in charge,
>just over two hundred
>>in a circle,
>>>knifed back
>>>>lest they grow into trees.

Mourners
>now in the
>>open
>>>pause in their
>>>>quarrel to
>>>>>relinquish

scrapes and
>tears,
>>understanding slowly
>>>veils will be lowered and
>>>>weddings fill with guests again,

(white squirrel nibbling by the gravestones
a symbol)

exclaiming over
>yellow forsythia sprays,
>>zealous to be held.

Part
TWO

SELECTED POEMS

From

THE RAINCOAT COLORS

2017

The Dead Keep Us Company

Now when we speak
they don't interrupt.

They let us win every argument
with nowhere to go,

nothing but time on their hands.
Our conspirators, they forgive

what we can't forgive ourselves,
that we didn't listen harder.

We can tell by their eyes
they have things to reveal.

We give ourselves over to them,
great organizers

of intimate information,
patient, letting us stand

at the counter
until we are ready to choose.

Off-hand, they tell us
what no one else
has the heart to.

Dedication

—Hotel des Invalides

You had planned a trip to Paris
before you died. I'm here in your place,
as you asked, my rooms overlooking
Rodin's rose garden
and, beyond, a city in itself,
the *Hotel des Invalides:* gilt basilica, military museums,
veterans asleep in upper wings—
missing you and your knowledge of history.

Napoleon's vault on a dias,
six coffins within coffins,
in the echoing rotunda.
I lean on the marble balustrade
and peer down, take it on faith,
inside, there was once
a husband and father.

It was hard to imagine
exile on Elba as punishment,
the air softened with lavender,
hot August on the soles of my feet
as we climbed the steps to his villa
the summer I was sixteen.
We saw the view of the sea his eyes fell on,
his writing desk, his pen set down
as though he had just left the room.
Who visits the island where he died,
stony Saint Helena?

I wish I could show you
the watercolors soldiers painted,
wash of green and blue
in a schoolboy's notebook,
faint pencil marks underneath:
World War I skirmishes
in farm towns with names
that belie the facts, lyrical,
Amiens, Champagne, Chemin des Dames,
towns we once drove through, speaking
this language I only half remember.

Down the *Invalides'* long blocks,
lined with cannons,
lies a tiny park where you took me
when we lived here in the '50's.
In a grove of chestnut trees,
a statue of Anatole France—
how the French revere their writers:
their names inscribed on street corners
to guide day-dreamy tourists.
I sit on a bench near a man who reads
as his daughter digs a leaf nest.
No one but you knows I'm here
in the shadow of the emperor.

The Garden Behind the Garden

*—At the Memorial for the Deported, Notre Dame
Cathedral, Paris*

Parvis: a garden enclosed behind a church.
Parvis, paradise, the same root.
Was there a fence around paradise, a wrought-iron gate
to be opened by a weighty key hanging
from an angel's belt?

Behind Notre Dame red roses grow along the Seine.
I never thought of paradise enclosed
but how else to keep Adam and Eve
from rattling the gate, trying to get back in?
This summer day, groups of tourists are visiting Notre Dame
but here none but me and a homeless man, asleep in a torn coat.

A policeman climbs the stairs to your apartment.
He holds a key, yells,
pack a suitcase and out, out, get to the station.

I never went down the steps to see the dimly lit cells
with the deported poets' words inscribed on the walls.
It was 1962. I started to go down
but my family was in a hurry
or I thought it was closed.

Or was I scared?
I tell myself I can go down another time.
It will be there.

I can count on it.

Adamantine

The word appeared on the page
from my pen.

I hadn't thought of it or spoken it.
A hard-headedness I kept coming up against
shimmered and beguiled.

Long ago confused
with the Latin *adamare*,

love, attachment,
both lodestone and magnet,

magnet and its opposite,
a legendary stone

of impenetrable hardness,
a diamond's diamond.

The word dared me
as I crawled through indecision.

I know *adamant*, fist on the table,
municipal, insistent,

but *adamantine* sees at night.
It shines in the centuries' dark,

reveals its facets from miles away
and inches from my face,

more anvil than star.
It can crush.

Luxembourg VIII

—After a lithograph by Harold Altman

Paris, late afternoon.
Two women walking.
They carry purses or shopping bags
away from sunlight
into the blue-gray graveled shadows.

The green trees close in. Green turns to black
beyond where the branches bend toward each other
over a handprint of sunlight.

I feel the relief of leaving the heat
but what am I stepping into?

Swings where my father pushed me
or I pumped myself, my legs pushing
higher and higher.

Fountains, reflecting pools,
and the *bateaux*
my brother sailed with sticks.

A block from the *jardins,* we lived in a small hotel
my mother tells me smelled of scalded milk.

A walk-up, the electricity kept going out
and the concierge shouted *Attention!*
I rode my red scooter in the courtyard.

This Paris, this park belong to the artist,
his own light and dark, shadow and brilliance,
as he plays with, rearranges Paris.

I can't, don't walk here, although
I can report the feeling of being alone
in this city, late in the afternoon,
when all the noise stops at once
as I turn a corner and enter a shaded *allée*,
eager for the luxury:

to go home and lie down for a minute,
before the evening begins
and extends into another day.

Thinking of the Anhinga

Beside the sand trap
like a bull fighter's cape
minus the crimson lining,
the anhinga spreads his wings to dry,
black feathers
dramatic, but not beautiful:
a mourning crepe.

It looks uncomfortable
the way he has to hold his wings
up and back
like a child being told
to stand up straight.

Grace in the awkward gesture—

Walking along on the grass
talking at cross purposes.

Submerged bird, a.k.a.
snakebird, water turkey, American darter,
only his long thin beak
juts above the surface, his plumage
not oiled, not waterproof.
Waterlogged, he stays under a long time.

Like a picnic cloth held above the grass,
the wings lift
like something about to happen
or that is always happening
or never quite does.

Falling asleep too early in the evenings.

They can be found
near standing water, by a canal,
beside a slash pine,
along the Naples city beach.

Severest drought in twenty years,
the fish-eater needs
water to dive into, needs to feed
at Lettuce Lake
in Corkscrew Swamp
with dangerously low
water levels: to find his spot on the bank,
beside the royal ferns, near the moon vine,
the cankerous green pond apples.

Not doing enough.
Doing too much too fast.

Like the monk in a saffron robe
at the self-serve gas pump,
the anhinga stands and dries his wings.

Prescription

On a scorched evening
under a full moon
one lone swimmer in the bay.

It could be you
shoulders relaxed,
buoyed on the waves.

When you visit the sea
you turn into the person
you thought you were.

First dreams don't always come true
and second, subsequent dreams,
what becomes of them?

When you visit the sea
you remember you want to live there,
as though you'd misplaced a longing

and now you want it written down,
to set in motion a reversal,
to quell your disposition.

Sand, swells, horizon,
evening's salt air in your lungs.
Longing will be key.

Interlude

As if waking up after years asleep

I open the book of painters from the Pacific Northwest:
Mark Tobey, Guy Anderson, Morris Graves,

their somber inkblot bouquets, their grays.
Here's Anderson's little still life—tendrils and stem—a marine
  blue vase,
a chair, perhaps a corner of his fishing shack
painted offhand, a jumble, where my afternoon expands

away from obligations.
Among these hues I breathe evenly for the first time in days,
admiring the ones whose dreams turned on turpentine, tobacco,
their lives contained in a few shades. Such serious men.
In the '40's they took the logging roads to paint from fire lookouts.

Heron-still, the pages unfold
with their beige, brown, black,
the raincoat colors.

Cascade

I wake up in a room with too many objects
tilting toward me: books, lamps, stacks of paper.

A world with countless things, how to make sense of it?
Some collect coins or orchids, depression glass,
many of one.

Bravery of those who wade into the swamp
in search of the rarest shoot,

diligence of the woman who found
200 sand dollars one morning on the beach,
insisting on perfection,
no broken edge.

Collecting shows signs of genius
my father said once, or more than once,
enough so that I haven't forgotten it,

and he used to talk, too, of collections that tip toward madness,
the Collyer brothers' stacks of newspapers
serpentined along their hallways.
Now it is a condition, has a name,
a diagnosis: hoarding.

And what of us, with our pieces
of green sea glass, (not the precious blue),
who can't focus enough
but can't begin to throw out,
caught like the things around us,
ticket stubs, beer coasters, French francs, a few of each.

Furnished Model

Every day he puts up the red and blue balloons
as if he's announcing a child's party

but it's a party of one,
a waiting game.

Who will walk in today and buy?
Who call?

Seeing him attach his balloons to the light pole
I'm not sad for him, but I understand

the daily work routines:
door key, light switch, desk drawer,

the effort to create an atmosphere
in a furnished model home

can wear a person down.
He has to smile. He has to shake your hand or mine

over the blueprints spread across his desk.
No clutter, not even a stray hair.

Anyone who walks in can imagine herself
conversing on the taupe sectional

or pulling the traverse rods
on the checkered window treatments.

No one is walking in.
His silver laptop sleeps among dust motes.

By dusk the balloons have shrunk
like hourglasses

and are drained of color
when he takes them down.

Dark Tasks, A Dream

Each night the riderless horse
appears, saddle strapped to his back,
stirrups flying, froth in his mouth,
lips pressed against his teeth.

No way to catch him, grab the reins,
as he careens into the yard
but I know it is my job.
I'm skittish, timid,
lack strength in my arms.
Don't panic.

Maternal instinct
tells me he can't be left to roam,
has to be reined in.
And I need
to dodge his kick,
bring him back to the barn.
I have no skills, no gift,
no *way* with a horse.

Where is the hot walker,
horse expert,
to cool him down, curry him,
walk him in the ring?

And the rider?
Is he someone
I've left behind?

Whatever I thought I once knew
how to do I've forgotten.

I try to coax the chestnut,
my palm up, empty.
He snorts and paws the ground.

I wish I knew what to say
to calm him.

I put down my whip,
pull on one boot.

He must be fed, but what?
Nothing picked from the garden,
nothing that can be named.

Time Travel

International Date Line:
a term learned in school,

dotted line on a map
I thought I would never cross.

Twenty four hours, an entire day away.
Mysterious as the equator

the Line divided day from day
day from night

the arbitrary way
the earth was split in half.

I learned Tuesday could be
Wednesday, a day gained or lost

depending how you traveled
most of a day spent in the air.

East or West.
Geography crossed into Math.

But how did I miss
knowing China has one time zone?

A friend who lives at the equator
tells me days up north

are too long or too short.
Hers are cut neatly in half.

The sun sets at seven
in a reassuring rhythm

as though rowing:
one oar in light, one in the dark.

A country was called Burma or Siam,
old names, when I shaded in the map

with colored pencils.
I'm searching for the simple

street or city, a date in history, syllables
to recite like stones I can hold in my hand

without ambiguity or ambivalence;
war assassination house arrest

pestilence or flood
become words like artifacts or curiosities.

My son now on the other side
of the International Date Line

revels in conveyances:
taxi, train, plane, motorcycle,

underground, ferry, bicycle, pedicab.
His passport's stamped

more than once a day,
its pages multiply,

visas, customs
he breezes through.

He knows the rules.
He reads the signs:

Do not wait for anybody.
Keep moving.

Direction

You would have known exactly what wind
swept across the parking lot this morning:
an engaging wind, not fierce, not the kind
to sting my ears or turn away from or combat,
to make me rush inside to my appointment.
It bent back the grasses by the railroad tracks
and carried a salt scent from the fields
miles inland from the sea.
I lingered in it, trying to determine
where it was coming from, southeast or west,
and who would have relied on it, or labored in it,
sailor or hunter, tensed to
a gust bringing rain on its back,
caught in a moment's feather-light maelstrom.

High Summer

I kept thinking of the phrase
as I walked, its transience, a trick

that lets me step outside
barefoot in light cotton

next to nothing
between indoors and out.

Did I come upon it
or did it envelope me?

A high point, a musical note
that holds.

A state or measure of time?
Time outside of time.

Some creatures estivate:
doze out the days

in their carapaces.
I am emboldened

egged on, reckless
ready to surrender,

up outside all night
elated. Anticipation

is another kind of carapace
as if I could breathe

underwater, forget it ends
as it begins.

From

THE GARDENER
AND THE BEES

2006

Perennial Bed

In September the bees spend hours
on the saucers of rose sedum,
their curled legs moving over petals
fleshy as rubber brushes.
I thought bees never stood still.
These hardly move,
becoming both the needle
and the painstaking fingers that hold them
until they cover each inch of tapestry.

This one lands on a filament
of coreopsis moonbeam,
floating down, down to the dirt
then flung back

through the undulating architecture.
Righting itself, it begins to investigate
the intricate netting, old bridal veil,
tiny yellow-tipped buds,
the ignored world at ankle level.

Down on my knees
I toil beside him and the others I see
hidden in the system of green stems.
I hum along, drawn in
by their noisy concentration.
Nothing gets in their way,
not my elbow, my shadow, my scent.
Let them sting me,
brash as I am.

Standing at the Trellis
Before Supper

It's always better to let someone
underestimate you.

Did the string bean say that?
Friend I didn't know I had,
staple of my great-grandparents' farm
in Foremost, Alberta.

Diligence. Industry.
Only now do I undertand
how they buckled down,
nose to the grindstone.

Blue Lake. Kentucky Wonder.
subtle but abundant
among its dusty vines, a military green,
now-you-see-it-now-you-don't,
like the brown egg that blends into the straw.

A cherry tomato named
Camp Joy, garden bauble,
shines pearl and silver green
as it ripens, tempting radiance,

but the bean hangs where it's always hung,
the garden's understatement,
unassuming, but vertical,
practical, plumb, a fact
like the pencil line I was taught
sails on into infinity.

Crabapple

In a plan to pare
I stared out the window:
how to make it round
like the trees on the hillside orchard.
In bed, anticipating
the outcome, the satisfaction
of the hauling away,
I felt the oiled shears in my hands,
the way I would wield them so vividly,
it might have been a dream at night
in which an entire act
is carried out to completion.

On that morning I turned
to lead limbs
outlined among gray clouds,
entered a hazy tunnel,
unable to follow a branch
in toward the trunk
or out to the tips
without getting lost.

My shears struck
resistant wood.
Each silvery twist
had a twin,
as though the severed shoots
kept growing back.
I still wait for instruction
from the patient
weight-bearing tree.

Crows in the Cul-de-Sac

The backyard's basic black
lives at the edge of things, like the deer,
not one to fly into deep wood
and vanish.

He likes a mown lawn,
chrysanthemum seed, my garbage,
happy with what we human beings
have done to North America,

staying close to a house
as he pecks, the way a child plays
by himself, while adults talk,
a child who learns to count
by counting crows.

The crow is my slip showing,
a run in my stocking,
late for the bus.

Two crows are sisters
who talk every day on the phone,
irritate each other across the wire
but don't hang up, discuss the little
details of their lives
no one else cares about.

Three crows conspire
near my neighbor's oak tree.

This is also my crow:
thumbprint on white paper,
shadow no one mentions,

a spot on the X-ray
the doctor says is nothing serious,
he'll just keep an eye on it,
a bird's eye.

Four crows figure
in proposition bets;
which one will fly off the fence first?

More than five crows gather
on the mossy oval
and I'm tempted to pull the shade
but I turn my head
and there's only one again,
my crow, my condition,
in the maple, the bare lilac branches.

Peonies

Rain has beaten the peonies.
They were standing tall yesterday,
top-heavy, guy-wired, half open in their hoops.

Now they spill on the asphalt,
stems bent, dragged down by their heads,
edges soiled,
exploded and scattered
beside the slender
controlled rose.

Petals litter the ground
like the morning after a gala-
someone has to clean up.
Peonies live large,
showy and glowing,
big guns of the suburbs.

They should not have been planted
on a slant above the driveway
but I won't move them now.
I have done what I have to
to keep them alive.

Cupping a bloom in my hands
I feel a pulse
as in a bird's body.

I've read that peonies thrive
for generations on old farms,
rain washing the soil down

from the cow pasture
to the gardens by the house.

As I walk from my car
I have only to brush against them
and they fall apart.

January

You left in the gray beginnings.

Animals slept underfoot.
Kings walked into the barn
two weeks late with gifts

and nothing could make it warm,
not my will or lists
of ways I would be better.

Time not to ask too much
of myself or others
but to bend to work at hand

the paths I had to shovel
and to walk along stone walls
snow covered

but I knew were there.

Coda

You used to say it ran in families,
this sense of time.
Your wristwatch glinting
beneath a crisp cuff
you set the standard
but it wasn't a strictness
you instilled, more of a personal attribute
like the way we smile
or move our hands when we talk.
It makes us feel better to be on time.

From the moment I heard you were sick
and I flew south
I fell behind.
When I arrived
they were already sweeping
your hospital room
preparing your bed
for someone else.

I thought I'd be at loose ends
yet even months later I feel
I will never catch up.
What I'm racing toward
is not the ocean liner
pulling away in a dream
but minutiae,
chores and purchases,
three calendars I mark
and forget to double check,
bills, letters, phone calls.

Why is it so satisfying
to cross out *milk*
or *dry cleaning,*
to gun my way
to the next errand?

I've forgotten what it's like
not to know what to do next.
Grief has become a bureaucracy.
I go through channels
to reach you.
I clutch my lists in line,
thinking of you,
your congeniality, your wit,
your traits become
small things written down.

Wedding Day

Out of the branches, inch-long bodies fell
all afternoon, softly, on the patio,
on the chairs and tablecloths
as the brown creatures stripped trees of green.
My father paid the grandchildren
a penny a bug to collect them.
The caterpillars don't appear in any pictures.
They never dropped in my hair
or landed on the neck of a guest,
or were caught in David's Mexican wedding shirt.
I like to think they slept through the ceremony,
stopped their work out of respect,
like gravediggers who lean on their shovels
to watch a wedding party pass.
They were there in the darkness of mid-June,
chewing through the reception, the music,
hardly a plague or an omen,
but a suburb's pestilence,
an arborist's headache,
part of the family lore, part of the story,
cobwebby, their fur petable,
the children not frightened
as they filled their buckets,
the insects' gauzy white tents
strung between the maples' limbs,
close to lovely from this distance.

Scrutiny

Years ago she was asked
to record her favorites
in the form of nouns:
blue, avocado, silk.
Now her list is private,
365 things to do:
hang the hummingbird feeder,
try to grow allium again,
make jello salad.
No one scrutinizes her desires.
The binoculars trained downstream,
she's left to fill in her own blanks
with a steady heartbeat.
At the old armory, de-toothed
and put to new uses,
the brick's right angles
assure her a place for her thoughts
like a doll cupboard
with 20 tiny drawers.
She asks nothing more
than to follow the signs
to the Commodore's House:
366th on her list.
Around the corner from the limelight:
her extended hyphenate of endeavors.

The Manatee Tank

Romaine lettuce heads float on the top of the tank,
every inch covered with leaves.
The tank is a study in green: green white
of the belly undersides, the lacy edge of leaves,
Sarasota sunlight spiraling down,
offering lime, moss, forest and sea
and the darker spruce shadows I stand in.

I wonder if the manatees like the hearts,
and how many heads a day they eat,
preferring iceberg,
though romaine is more nutritious.
I've also leaned at the kitchen counter,
tearing off leaves, mindlessly chewing.
That must be what we have in common,
a shared love of salad
and the talent to pass hours
nibbling, adrift.

The teenage girls who crowd the glass beside me
squeal that these thousand-pound mammals
brushing past the glass are trying to kiss them.
The girls want to kiss back,
or climb in and stroke the slippery sides
of Hugh and Buffet, of the order Sirenia,
pat the pink heads and flippers, tails an afterthought.

I imagine the girls also have the know-how
to idle away an afternoon,
lying on pillows across the living room floor,
brushing their hair, the strands
rising up in the light as if it were water,
while their mothers who shoo them out, to accomplish,
not to waste the best part of the day,
to breathe fresh air, may have forgotten
the desire to be suspended safely in bodies
so odd they endear themselves to the world.

At the Feeder

The sound of running water
draws the hummingbird she says
as she stirs sugar water,
fills the feeder by the fuchsia near the kitchen
where she stands at the sink,
her day organized
around the bird's arrival.

A minute shift in light
signals he's there,
blur of a blur, suspended
on the other side of the screen
a few inches from her face,
her companion shadow.

What can I call her? Resigned . . . stoic?
Patience makes her at home
in the care she shows
rinsing a dish, her feet
steady on clean linoleum

drawing strength from
the way she was raised
to be frugal,
to attend to detail:
the correction, the counter shift
at the window
as he whirs away.

From

THE CANAL BED

1985

The Hunt

—Shuyak Island, Alaska

I touch the pelt nailed to the wall,
black tail, black stripe along the spine.
I want to pull it over my shoulders
and walk out, bare feet burning
on the icy streets.

After you shot the buck,
you had to shoo away three deer,
which sat beside it.
Wind blew toward your face.
We left the head in the moss,
eyes black and glassy.

Last night I went back for the skull,
picked clean in tundra snow.
It spoke but soil absorbed its words.
What I held was your head,
hollowed in tundra air.
I knew I would leave my body
next to yours.

Turning in sleep
I saw the deer stand up again,
sheathed in sunlight as you shouted.
Lifting their heads in the wind
they blinked, their eyes not quite believing.

Artifacts

Wind blows from the mainland across the Straits,
over nettle-covered middens where we've dug
for Aleut arrowheads, unearthing
fishbones, clam shells, human teeth.

Tribes slept near these hills
and in daylight told of omens dreamed
as salmon, startled elk.

Trout broach, eagles circle
yet never enter my sleep.
I thought out here the mind would empty
and be filled as quietly as sky with stars.

When I close my eyes I see torn sheets and blackboards.
I want the spruce, sea otter, cormorant
inside of me to speak.

Sitka Spruce

Blacker than water, branches churn,
blades in a hard wind,
timber so dark I want to
peel back the bark, expose
the white meat of wood,

or follow the ways of old tribes
that weakened trees with fire.
Flames smoldered around a trunk
for weeks as they chipped away with stones.
One log held forty whale hunters
clutching their spears.

Without tools, with no idea
how to turn a forest into oars,
I walk the beach gathering deadfall.
Trees blanched by tidal waves
lie on their sides, roots thrust in the air.
I break off branches and carry what I can.

Bread

Dough rises in the sun,
history of the human race inside it:
orgies, famine, Christianity,
eras when a man could have his arm
chopped off for stealing half a loaf.
I punch it down, knead the dark
flour into the light, let it bake,
then set it on the table beside the knife,
learning the power
cooks have over others, the pleasure
of saying *eat.*

The Mountains of
Ten Thousand Smokes

When I row I feel them closing in.
Through fog they're wisps,
barely visible, photographs of the soul.
If the sun sends down its spokes,
peaks rear from the ocean,
hard white folds disgorging mists.

They shift their weight
when I blink, as if they might
rise up or sink and take me with them.

The boat floats forward, its prow
Like two hands pressed together.

Ghosts in the Garden

Last winter we walked through the supermarket,
slush on our boots,
shocked by the price of melon.

You remembered luncheons
your mother gave in Seattle:
honeydew, prosciutto, strawberries.
You left as soon as you were twenty.

The summer I stayed with her
I stood on the lawn while she hosed
her rhododendrons.
We sat on the porch,
wisteria blowing around us.
She played gin with my grandfather.

On visits East they stayed at the Waldorf.
We went out to dinner, the theater,
my grandmother in cool black furs, jewels,
smelling of lemon blossom.

Back home you brooded in our garden,
tossed cigarette butts in the flower beds.

This evening I arrive for dinner.
Her china shines on your table.
Azalea and aster envelop the yard.
The sprinkler turns through sunlight
as though a hand with diamonds on it
flashed across the lawn.

The Roses

In the late afternoon,
wearing gloves, my mother
bends to pour bone meal
on the flower beds
until every inch
of earth is white.
Each year more roses
surround the house.

Last August I was sick.
She brought me the Mojave,
her prize rose.
When the wind blew,
petals drifted
on my wrists, across the sheets,
curled and dry
as insect husks.

Every winter my father hands her
roses, awkwardly unburdening
himself. And she accepts,
placing the stilt-like stems
in water by the window.
Against the bald sky
those dark formal flowers
unfold.

Housekeeping

The woman down the street
hangs out her clothes like paintings:
Monet's violet-flowered sheets,
the Grant Wood of her husband's jeans,
tiny T-shirts and pink socks: Paul Klee.

They smell of sunlight when she reels them in,
folds back sleeves like wings
and smooths the sheets shyly
as if touching her husband.

Outside, leaves keep falling.
They cover her yard, so many,
such odd shapes, if only
she had drawers for them
or could mail them out likes bills.

Everywhere underground lie
bulbs she buried at random,
like balled-up socks in a drawer,
forgotten under the dark snow,
until the crocuses surprise,
objects she thought she'd lost:
combs, mirrors, cups, brilliant
spools unwinding.

The Institutions on our Block

Who knows what's worshiped in this temple?
Two nights a week men file in
leaving wives and children behind.
They wear suits and ties.
They mumble secret chants about brotherhood,
Masons, sharpening tools
more mysterious than the mortician

next door, enveloped in wisteria.
He hides his clean, black limousines,
leaves two lamps on all night,
curtains parted, shadows cast
as in a dim boudoir.

Up on the hill the hospital hums
with life-support systems:
X-rays, brain scans, probes
that tell the sex of the baby,
the size of the cyst,
enough morphine locked in its cupboards
to put this town to sleep.

I still tell the seasons
by staring at the grade-school windows.
Today thirty turkeys are pasted to the glass.
The panes wait for snowflakes and hearts.
Planets hang in the main hall,

a luminous mobile, Pluto,
and Saturn's pale yellow rings.
Maps of the world are nailed to the doors,
rivers flowing in red ink.

At three o'clock children walk out
of the building, up the street,
wearing black pointed hats
and feathered headdresses,
their lips buzzing with new facts.

The Canal Bed

*—Built in 1793, the Middlesex Canal ran from
Lowell to Charlestown, Massachusetts*

The canal has been abandoned
and found again
by antiquarians
walking the side roads
up to their knees in leaves.
Some sections still fill
with water, others lie
buried under roads.

You grew up here.
When the guidebook says it passed
through the softball diamond at Foss Park,
under Boston Avenue Bridge,
between Wedge and Winter duck ponds
you see traffic lights,
graffiti scrawled above the railroad tracks.

I trace its course along the map,
picturing scenes from old engravings:
boats loaded with coal,
Baptists immersing themselves,
skaters circling bonfires,
and Woburn, where the first Baldwin apple
was grafted by the colonel
who ran the canal
until the railroad wiped it out.

Picknickers rode packet boats
to the Lake of the Woods:
"The sun set, the moon rose,
the band played
and gentlemen sang songs."

❖

You snap your wrist,
the line flies out.
You lean the pole
against a rock and wait,

part of the twilight.
I stand beside you
watching for rainbow trout
to rise in silver rings.

We do not speak or touch,
our eyes drawn
to the surface the sun
fills with purple as it sinks

half in, half out of water.

It took eight hundred hours
to build the boat by hand,
gray, with black shutters,
moored by the old Baldwin house
on a half-mile stretch of water.

Sundays they offer rides.
The day we went, the horse,
stung by a bee, bolted back
across the highway
through the shopping center
to the barn.

Our wide flat street
is part of the old towpath.
At night I imagine water
flowing beside us, hooves,
cargo hauled to Boston.

Instead, dazed teenagers dare
each other: they knock down
trash cans, stone walls,
hide in the shrubs
until the police leave.

Honeysuckle shrouds the canal
near Baldwin Street in Lowell,
but straight ahead roll
the Merrimack's broad waters.

No place to sail.
We'd have to stop at the dam,
portage through the parking lot
of Archambault's funeral parlor.

Better to stand on the bridge,
stare at rocks slippery
with moss or over our shoulders
where the river widens
and at dusk turns an oily rose.

A door bangs in my sleep.
I should set it on the water
like a raft.

How far could I go
before I ran aground,
reached Black Brook Lock,
no one in the tollhouse to open it?

This is the way excursions end:
railroad tracks stop in a field,
the road curves into someone's yard.

What can we do but get out and walk,
leave the canoe,
carry the camera and picnic basket,

straggle through twilight arguing
who misread the map,
took the wrong turn,

or else sit down in a field,
eat the remains of lunch,
pretend we are waiting for help,
pretend help never comes.

Always by water—
the Concord, Shawsheen,
Aberjona,

small pools,
or the Atlantic's
violent wake—

walking by water
brings us close.

Here are photographs we took
last year in Wilmington
in the ruins of an aqueduct.

Gray clouds drifted
between the trees
like ghostly undersides of boats.

Wild grapevines grazed our heads.
Roots burst from stone.

The Riverbank

When you see a speck in the sky
you cry *bird*.
You haven't learned *swallow* or *crow*.
A stalk of ryegrass
you call *flower*.

What you drink from your cup,
what falls from the sky,
what flows past us now is *water*.
You don't know *river, rain,* or *tear,*
or the *rough gray-green* reflected beside us.

Trust me when I say we're surrounded
by air. It carries *baby* and *backpack,*
but the word you hear me sing
so often, *love*, seems spoken
by a mother in a book
leaning to another child.
Hand feels truer. *Branch. Stone.*

To you the word is one more sound.
You point to the setter across the river
as if you could touch him.
I'm holding you when I say
love. Do you hear me, far away?

Dogs Named After Islands

When we call our dogs we are honoring
volcanoes, the continental drift,
God's casual hand in creation.

They race towards us like boats
steering between islands,
a wake of insects and weeds.

We call back places
we'd like to settle in
but never will,

a windy Alaska portage,
a shack on Puget Sound,
our boots rattling gray stones
shaped like totems:

Shuyak   Vashon

Strangers struggle with the syllables,
humoring us, as if we had named
our children after trees.

Asleep they curl like islands
seen from the air.

Often, thinking of something else,
we touch them as if
trailing our hands in water.

From the Same Cloth

—For the mill girls, Lowell, Massachusetts,
circa 1840

The city fathers dreamed these girls
the way they dreamed the town:
to scale, pale colors on a map, dolls
bending at looms by day, reading
the classics by night. Now I imagine them
as they rise to bells, break ice
in washing bowls, file at dawn
to the mills, their breath pouring before them.

All day they stand, each girl
at a different task: to guide raw
cotton through the spindle, blend dye
for yellow calico, count each bolt
for dish towels, sheets, their future husbands'
shirts, their own petticoats.
They hear machines roar the way the river
roars, breast wheels turning.

Do they whisper sonnets to themselves
or think of Cleopatra on the Nile,
clay banks where men lie sleeping?
Do they dream of being loved like that?

Each time a girl writes home, part of her
follows the letter across the border
to New Hampshire, growing damp
as it nears the sea, then safe,
unfolded by her mother's hands.

When she places her cheek on cold cotton
she sees the years ahead
like yards of undyed linen,
and yearns to watch a warehouse full
of dimity catch fire.
She wants to walk past the row
of beds, down to the river's most
seductive bend, to lie on the grass,
wet blades staining her nightgown,
feeling the hush, the sound
of nothing being made.

The Abandoned Mill

To a woman driving by at night
the mill seems more like home
than the houses she passes,
their cheerful army of lamps
inviting yet sending her away.

She remembers how she walked here
as a child, her hands stretched out, in shadow.
She came because she might get hurt
or lost so far her friends
would never find her, stepping into the mirror
and never coming back.

She breathed the spidery smell,
found the best corners
for an echo, shouting as she
wanted to in church,
rubbing the floors worn hollows.

Tonight, beside black walls, black
windows, black sky, black water,
she lets the darkest part of her lie down.

By the Merrimack

I walk a path built of granite,
wooden rail at the level of my hand.
I want to follow the entire river
as it flows through names
I've seen on maps: Manchester, Concord,
city of peace, of smooth, fat grapes,
and the villages: Tilton, Riverhill.
I'd pass each in one stride
until I reached the first
drop of water as it fell.

I could continue to the corner
where New Hampshire narrows,
darkens, its houses sparse,
and this river's sister,
the Connecticut, begins.

Or I could walk the other way.
No one knows where the river
ends, the ocean starts.
As a child I tried to pinpoint the spot,
believing I could find a seam,
a line of sunlight on the current
between fresh water and salt.

It's like the place one falls
in and out of love: now sharp,
now sweet, the wrists
plunged in, the same
steady pressure of longing or regret.

AFTER CURFEW

From

PERSONAL EFFECTS

1976

Midas' Daughter

Before my father died outcast
in Eden, choked by gold lapels
he cried for blood and butterflies.
He'd picked his kingdom clean.

I hacked the gilt for dirt
to bury him. Gloss ran too deep.
I put him in his garden
dead beside the dagger lilies.

I inherited his greed,
but not for gold—I'd slept
in solid sheets of it—I fled
the polish of his world for one

where I could work my heart and fingers
to the bone. I asked for it.
Now everything I touch breaks
into tears or flame.

Evening Chores

The garden is growing smaller.
Roses merge with gravel
as the sun withdraws.
This is twilight's ashen grace.
For a moment we face each other
without suspicion, features softened.
Our bodies press against the window
as if to steer this house
across the sinking hills.
Lights flicker in the distance.
Roofs slide away
like clothes into drawers.
We turn back to our tasks
becoming, whites of eyes,
a shoulder blade
a shirt and a blouse full of wind.

Morgue

Each body is a blue carnation
in a long white box,
odorless
as florist-cooled flowers.
They glow
in their greenhouse of flesh
as if lit miles
below the surface
by rose lamps.
Their veins are moths
frozen in that light.
Sound-proofed,
surrounded by dials,
the dead drift
between grief
and earth.

Raccoon Skeleton at
Long Plain Creek

Wading upstream we bump his carcass
with our ankles. He jiggles
like the needle of a compass
scattering silt until he's pure
milk white.
Tin shines through his skull.
He soaks light
right through his sockets.
Water runs its tongue
inside his crevices. We link
fingers, looking down . . .
all the soft things are gone,
bone gets its turn.

Selected
EARLIER POEMS

Butterflies on an Illinois Road

the world is the color of pumpkins
the dirt along the road runs like cider
corn stands up straight in green fields when
  butterflies hundreds of butterflies
    the colors of lemons
 and rust
    the colors of oranges
 and emeralds
      striped
        silver
         gold
          black
 butterflies
    suddenly fly by
       the windshield
banging their bare shoulders
on the car

The Shoes

You were thirteen, in an era when women still changed purses
every season and wore white gloves to church.
The boxes piled up like Christmas
as you studied the grays and browns.
Why did you feel so sad staring at your feet?

Your mother said, *Choose*,
and you stepped, by instinct,
into the pair with the pert bow.
Your pink feet swelled like yeast dough
over the leather edges.

In arithmetic you learned
that a woman wearing heels
exerts a pressure of a thousand pounds.
You walked softly, to withhold your weight from the earth.

Homesick

I am sent to visit Dorothy,
my mother's friend
on Bainbridge Island.

What to do with me?
She has three sons, no daughter.
A short drive to a saltwater pool.

Cold, gray, the pines close in
over concrete, a military feel,
her sons all

somersaults and cannonballs.
I shiver on the edge,
miss kicking in the blue

of pools I'm used to.
She hands me a hula hoop,
the rage in 1958.

Out on the lawn after dark
the hoop glows bubblegum pink.
It circles down in the grass

as I twist and sway,
try to set a record for how long
I can keep it in the air around my waist.

Saugatuck

the name of the river
that ran below our house,
the name of my school
and the village across the bridge
where the train stopped
and my mother met my father every evening.

Next to the school,
our house on Bridge Street
stood red as a nightshirt,
in a stand of oak.
My teachers' names came back
to me last night in conversation:
Mr. Melillo, Mrs. Dunagan, Coach Dorsey.

In kindergarten kind Mrs. King
fed us graham crackers and orange juice,
the most sober ambrosia.
The boys wore Keds, the girls
saddle shoes and red barrettes.

All morning we went
from corner to corner
to drop a plastic coin
in the toy register
or stir oatmeal for a doll.
We didn't mind
doing what we were told.

At the Construction Site
of the Hydro-electric Plant

—Lowell, Massachusetts, 1984

The whistle blows its warning:
one minute before dynamite.
Students leave their desks
to watch the ground cave in.
They are so used to television
they want to see it all again
to know what really happened.
They joke about a dorm exploding,
the whole campus, classes cancelled,
but underneath the laughter
who among them did not feel
the earth break
the riverbank shudder and collapse?

Crossing the bridge after class,
one boy looks down at the river, rushing, white,
and thinks of it held back, released,
as if a bolt were thrown
and stallions charged to drive the turbines.
Pulsing currents, a tremor
in the fingertips and soles of the feet.
The sight of water often moves him
more than any human being.

What is it like to lay the sticks
and light the fuse? To try it once—
the way he hits the wedge
and wood splits open at his feet.
a clean break, down the middle, the echo
of the axe—
to make the windows tremble
without shattering.

Lunch Hour Line

During an inquiry
about metal awning specs,

the wooden floor creaks
under the City Clerk.

Next a petition
for the Sign Review Board.

She opens the Code,
green, bound, chained to the counter.

Trained in ways to defuse anger,
she works her own

in the hard candy she sucks,
the sweater clip she re-adjusts,

the eye she gives her co-workers
as one more citizen, satisfied or not,

turns his back and leaves the room,
shadow receding behind frosted glass.

Each time the door opens
the parochial schoolchildren's cries

echo off old brick and asphalt,
over the roofs of the empty convent,

around the corner of the credit union,
rattling the funeral parlor windows.

Out in the hall marble plaques
list the Civil War dead.

Upstairs the flag, the stage,
the microphones wait

for *testing, testing*
of the city councilors.

Why does it have to be so difficult
to post a sign or pave a driveway?

These are questions it's ok to ask
a stranger waiting beside me,

to befriend with body language:
eye-roll, watch-check, whispered aside.

Bureaucracy is about getting along
at noon in the middle of the week.

Standing close, wrist brushing
wool, I note the need

for breath mints, smell oil
on the mechanic's jacket, in line for

dog license, burn permit,
tax abatement, block party.

The bell rings, the children
go inside to their seats,

leaving an abrupt silence,
in which we shift, chastened,

as the air in the high-ceilinged room
changes shape around us.

A new petitioner steps forward,
my turn to face the Clerk.

Working Meditation

We're trying to fix the computer
until I notice Beth's silver necklace
with the geometric turquoise design
she brought back from Santa Fe last year.
Clark points out his Zuni ring
he bought at a rodeo
in North Platte, Nebraska, 1975.
I remember Ogallala, as I drove through
in September, 1977, east to west.

Willa Cather, he says, unplugging the mouse
(I'm glad the flowers in her books—
Bleeding Heart, Shasta Daisy—
live on in my garden).

Ogallala he observes,
unscrewing the motherboard,
is where the cattle *dead head*.
He's taught us a new, technical term,
To make a return trip without a load.
In Webster's, he says, it follows
dead hand (mortmain),
the oppressive influence of the past,
as he jiggles the keyboard.

What of sleight of hand,
I want to ask, the way we smile here,
not giving ourselves away.

What of the way a hand's light touch
re-awakens the screen,
or how so many of us flaunt
the nontechnical side of the brain,
or of the ringless hand
that passed over the sleeping head,
the child grown, the bed empty.

Clark takes the hard drive;
he can't get it going today.
Beth has memos to type.
Her hand pats the necklace
to make sure it's still there,
against her chest.

I'm left in the workroom to ponder
the gaps between milestones,
how, on summer evenings,
while computers sleep,
the middle-aged are caught
staring into space, wondering why we arrived
on these flagstones, under this salt of stars,
this sickle moon, delicate as a bracelet charm,
sharp enough to cut.

Ballardvale

Asked to sketch a village, a child draws
this place where the train stops
near the post office, corner store,
cottage converted for the dentist's drill.
Hats and boots at the fire station
wait for the alarm.
Playground swings stand
stock still.
In the matchstick apartment
a man leans
as if prepared to
somersault over the rail.
The dam is full to the brim
like a cup even two hands
can't keep from spilling
down to a father and son
gently maneuvering
a blue canoe.

Smoke rises from a house
that might have been
where the poet lived
a year or two
when she was young.
No one knows much about her
early life; the child doesn't
as she traces the mint-green car,
one of many vehicles
that pass through here
morning and evening
from driveway to boulevard
and back, sending
the white cat into the lilacs.

Writing Through:
A LIFE IN POETRY

Writing Through: A Life in Poetry

I was a teenager when I wrote my first poems. I grew up in a house full of books. My father was a writer. My mother taught French. We often read aloud together as a family, and a favorite family parlor game was "In the Manner of the Word," where we had to act out an adverb. My father's mother, Alice, was terrific at this game, a natural actress.

Poetry was "taught" to us in elementary school. Seamus Heaney, when he spoke in Lawrence, Massachusetts, under the auspices of the Robert Frost Foundation, described the difference between the poetry you learn in school and that which you discover on your own. In fifth grade, I memorized "Stopping by Woods on a Snowy Evening," and stood in the front of the room to recite it. How many thousands of American children have also stood and recited this poem?

In seventh grade we read *The Looking Glass Book of Verse*, an anthology of children's poetry, edited by Janet Adam Smith. I still have my copy. Inside the front cover I had made a list, in ink, titled, "Important Poems." The page number of each poem is listed, followed by a check mark. The list begins with "On First Looking into Chapman's Homer" by John Keats. I remember being puzzled by the syntax of the title. What did it mean to "look into" "Chapman's Homer," as though it were a box, with a lid? It strikes me now as a very abstract poem to be included in an anthology of children's poetry, and that initial sense of bewilderment has lingered all these years when I read this poem. Some of the other twenty-five Important Poems were, not surprisingly, Frost's "Stopping by Woods," as well as "The Runaway," Yeats' "An Irish Airman Foresees his Death," Wordsworth's "Westminster Bridge." A list of Important Poems for me today might include Robert Frost's "Directive," which I did not discover until years after I left school, "The Lane" by Edward Thomas, "October" by Louise Glück and "A Benign Self-Portrait" by M. Scott Momaday, and the list might change next week.

Writing is a solitary pursuit but most writers usually seek out at least a few people with whom they share their interest in poetry, along with their own work. My first, and one of my most heady experiences with a group of writers, was during my senior year in high school, when I was part of the editorial board of the school literary magazine. Every Friday afternoon we met in the basement of the administration building to read and discuss work that had been submitted. Submissions were anonymous and left in a box on our advisor's desk. We took our charge seriously. Sometimes the work under discussion had been written by one of us, and we had to sit and listen to comments without reacting. I admired and respected the other members of the group. This was one of my favorite parts of the week, an hour out of time, an idyll.

I was fortunate, in my twenties, to have the opportunity to attend graduate school in the MFA writing program at the University of Massachusetts, in Amherst, another idyll. There, for two years, my fellow students and I immersed ourselves in writing and we were given permission to think of poetry as the most important undertaking in the world. There were moments when I wondered what people did with their time when they didn't write. I found out soon enough, when life opened up—or closed off—in other ways, with work and daily obligations.

I have been part of an ongoing writing workshop, for years now, with a group of poets with whom I can share my work, as well intermittently part of other groups. There are also a few individuals on whom I count to tell me what does and doesn't succeed in a poem. My fellow poets and I used to meet at each other's kitchen tables. Lately we are more likely to share our poems by email and by Zoom. No matter the method, these interactions are crucial to my writing.

William Stafford once said that part of being a writer means accepting the stages you're going through. By that I think he meant if you're going to be a writer you will need to "write through" various moments, carry on, whatever comes your way, have patience with yourself. Sometimes a poet writes more than at other times; sometimes poetry feels more central to a life than at others. You may not even know until looking back later what the stage was you were going through.

Notes

Paris Paint Box

Preface, "a painter of the early morning light," Rey, 1982, p. 15.

Part I, Opening quotation, Guichard, Higonnet, p. 19.

"Berthe Morisot with a Fan," Edouard Manet, in a letter to Fantin-Latour, Higonnet, p.59.

The Harbor at Lorient, Higonnet, p. 62.

"The Militia Billeted in the Studio," Marie-Cornélie Morisot, Rouart, P. 72; Morisot, Rouart, p. 54; "Kisses for Bibi . . ." Rouart, p. 55.

"Fédéric Bazille," Berthe to Edma, Rouart, p. 61.

"Correspondence," ". . . one always derives benefit . . . " Berthe to Edma, Rouart, p. 52.

"I have never . . . " Edma to Berthe, Rouart, p. 32.

"Questions for Mr. Darwin," Berthe, letter, Rouart, p.90.

"The Wedding Ring," "no confidence," Higonnet, p. 82; "honest and excellent," Higonnet, p.119.

Part II, opening quotation, "This woman who seemed all her life . . . " Rey, 1982, p. 90.

"Stéphane Mallarmé," "Laertes," Rouart, p. 203 and 206; quatrain, Rouart, p. 208.

"friendly Medusa," *The Paris Review,* Madison Mainwaring, July 2019, online.

"The Abandoned Book," The poet Stéphane Mallarmé was considered the father of Hypertext, Poetry Foundation, online.

"Julie," "pink in the light . . ." Higonnet, p. 192.

Self-Portrait, "military and abrupt," Lloyd, p.133.

"Miss Cassatt and Mlle. Morisot," "Wanting to capture . . ." Higonnet, p. 203; "shameless hussy," Higonnet, p.124.

Portrait of Berthe Morisot, "real wall of ice . . . " Higonnet, p. 172.

"Conversations with Eugène," "Thonjoun—Turkish . . . for lamb," Higonnet, p. 119; " . . . surface of a heart . . . " Higonnet, p. 209; "Dover . . . Calais . . ." Higonnet, p. 209.

"'We All Die with Our Secret,'" from Morisot's unpublished journal, Higonnet, p. 220.

"An Art of Absence," "Give your cousin . . ." Higonnet, p. 221; "irritated melancholy," Lloyd, p. 133.

BOOKS CONSULTED:

Berthe Morisot, Anne Higonnet, Berkeley and Los Angeles: University of California Press,1995.

Berthe Morisot, Jean-Dominique Rey, Paris: Flammarion, 2010, 2018.

Berthe Morisot, Jean-Dominique Rey, New York: Crown Publishers, 1982.

Berthe Morisot, The Correspondence with her Family and Friends: Manet, Puvis de Chavannes, Degas, Monet, Renoir, and Mallarmé, Denis Rouart, ed., London: Moyer Bell Ltd., 1987.

Growing Up with the Impressionists: The Diary of Julie Manet, Julie Manet, New York: I.B. Tauris, Ltd., 2017.

Mallarmé: The Poet and His Circle, Rosemary Lloyd, Ithaca, N.Y.: Cornell Univ. Press, 2005.

"Direction" from *The Raincoat Colors* is for David. "Dedication," from T*he Raincoat Colors,* and "Coda," from *The Gardener and the Bees,* are in memory of my father, Robert William Minton. "The Roses," from *The Canal Bed,* is in memory of my mother, Lal Minton.

A Note on the Author

Helena Minton's previous collections include *The Canal Bed* with Alice James Books, *The Gardener and the Bees* with March Street Press, and *The Raincoat Colors* with Finishing Line Press. Her poems have appeared in a variety of journals and anthologies, including *The Beloit Poetry Journal, Ibbetson Street, The Listening Eye, Sou'wester, Poetry, West Branch, Nasty Women Poets: An Unapologetic Anthology of Subversive Verse,* and *Raising Lilly Ledbetter: Women Poets Occupy the Workspace.* She worked for many years as the director of a public library, and has also taught English Composition and Creative Writing. She has an MFA in Creative Writing from the University of Massachusetts/Amherst and serves on the Board of the Robert Frost Foundation, in Lawrence, Massachusetts. She lives north of Boston.